Weekly Reader Books presents

Cranes in My Corral

DAYTON O. HYDE
Cranes in My Corral

Pictures by Lorence Bjorklund

The Dial Press · New York

To those who cannot fly

Cranes in My Corral

1

The day the sandhill crane eggs hatched was the day my cowboys quit in disgust. I was so excited to discover the eggs chipping open that I rushed right over to where the men were saddling their horses to share the good news. The thought of a grown man being interested in birds was too much for them. The two almost swallowed their chewing tobacco.

Turned back by their silent stares, I wheeled about and dashed back to the eggs. With trembling hands I gently lifted each bantam-chicken foster mother off her adopted egg and peeked beneath. First came tiny holes in the shells of the big, brown mottled eggs. At the tip of each little rubbery beak a sharp, flinty egg tooth jerked and hammered time and again at the prison wall of the eggshell, chipping away until the caps of the eggs tipped back like trap doors and let the crane chicks squirm forth, scrawny and wet from their own body wastes. Two eggs hatched, then two more, and I found myself the father of four golden-brown, gosling-sized baby sandhill cranes.

The jingle of cowboy spurs ended my concentration.

"Birds!" snorted Reata Slim in disgust as he stormed up the front steps of the bunkhouse.

"Eggs!" growled his saddle pal, Blister Bill. "You can be doggone sure the only eggs I was ever forced to be around was properly fried."

Even their half-broken-in mustangs seemed to stare across the field at me in pity. The two old cowboys packed up their bedrolls, shook the trail dust from their faded neckerchiefs, and took off at a high lope for town.

I didn't blame the men. It was pride that made them hire out to work at Yamsi, my uncle's rough, tough cattle ranch at the headwaters of the William-

son River in southern Oregon. Now pride was making them leave again. My uncle Buck, from whom I had bought the ranch, was a crusty, do-it-the-old-way cattle rancher, and I guess when the men agreed to stay on working for me they expected me to continue his Wild West traditions. The big difference between my uncle and me was that besides ranching I happened to be interested in birds.

Sandhill cranes are long-legged marsh birds standing chest high to a six-foot cowboy, with wing-spreads exceeding a grown man's reach. At a distance they are a soft pearl gray; close up one notices immediately the lovely rose skin on forehead and crown. Numerous in covered-wagon days, their great trumpeting voices were part of the sound and the fury of the lonely West. Market hunters took the first toll; now drainage of their marshy nesting grounds has hastened the species toward possible extinction. Only their smaller cousins, the lesser sandhill cranes, which nest unmolested in the far north, are still in abundance. The sandhill's great sonorous, rusty voice, rolling out over the marshes, is as rare now as the rumble of moving buffalo herds or the squeal of wooden wagon wheels.

Four years before, I had hatched a sandhill crane from an egg rescued from a flooding, ice-choked stream. The crane, a female we named Sandy, had grown up as a member of our family and now, of breeding age at last, had found a mate somewhere in the marshes and laid two eggs in the calf pasture. When Sandy showed more interest in following me about the ranch than in incubating her eggs, we gathered them up and placed each egg under a broody bantam chicken. Sandy promptly laid two more, which she also ignored.

These eggs too went under chicken foster mothers. I had dreams of building a captive flock, of learning enough about raising sandhill cranes in captivity that I might rebuild the wild population, thus saving them from extinction. But since no books were available on how to raise sandhill cranes, I would have to learn as I went along.

For the moment my experiment seemed to be paying off. Wild sandhills hatch only two chicks; by the time they raise these two, tending them dutifully, it is too late in the season to raise another brood. Now under captive conditions, by gathering the eggs and relieving the parents of the tedious responsibility of raising the young, I had increased production. Never before in recorded history had four sandhill cranes been raised in one season from a single pair of parent birds.

"What on earth will you name them?" my wife asked, a little nervously as though she too found it

strange that a cattle rancher could be interested in birds.

"Name them?" I asked. "Why not call one Choo Choo Crane, and another Ichabod Crane after the character in Washington Irving's 'The Legend of Sleepy Hollow,' and then—"

My wife groaned. "How about Eeny, Meeny, Miney, and Moe?"

"Preep!" called Eeny, largest of the chicks.

"Preep!" cried Meeny, who was almost as large.

"Preep!" said Miney, next in line.

But poor little Moe said nothing at all. Smaller than the rest, just as he was about to go "Preep!" he stubbed his toe and fell flat in the water dish.

Moe wasn't much to look at, but fortunately his adoptive mother thought him quite the handsomest baby "chicken" she had ever seen. But then maybe she was ready to accept anything. The previous summer, when a raven stole her eggs from a nest hidden on a shelf in the blacksmith shop, she had spent her days trying in vain to incubate three pebbles, four marbles, a piece of bubble gum, and a golf ball autographed by the President. She clucked to Moe in deep contentment, and soon he was nestled deep in the soft warmth of her feathers, none the worse for his dunking.

But content as the chicks seemed, there was

nevertheless the problem of getting them to accept food. For two days after hatching, as they absorbed the remnants of their yolk sacs, the soft, downy chicks seemed bound and determined to starve themselves to death. Then, one by one, they learned to take bits of crushed earthworm from my fingers. Soon they were not only eating by themselves from a dish, but were growing fast.

Though Eeny, Meeny, and Miney quickly adjusted to pen life, Moe was soon in trouble again. On the floor of his pen he discovered what looked like the biggest, fattest, juiciest worm, right beneath his beak. He glanced around hastily, perhaps thinking that a bigger chick might come along and take it from him. Hardly believing his good luck, he cocked his head and regarded the worm with one big brown eye. It seemed so tame, almost friendly.

"Preep!" Moe said proudly, seized it with his bill, and straightened up tall.

But alas! It wasn't a worm at all but his own middle toe. This time Moe landed flat on his back in the food trough.

2

For several days the four little cranes were content with their foster mothers, and the hens loved them as though they were their very own. Each crane was in a separate pen to keep him from fighting with his brothers and sisters, but in the afternoons they were let out for a stroll. They ate worms, gobbled bugs, chased dragonflies across the meadow, stared in wonder at butterflies, and grew and grew until, as was inevitable, they began to outgrow their mothers.

At night they flopped down, long legs folded beneath them, while the hens settled happily over them to ward off the chill of the night. But now and then, lured by some irresistibly fascinating noise, a little sandhill crane head would periscope up through the feathers of his mother's back. As the crane rose higher and higher on his stiltlike legs, the mother would rise up with him until, with an angry squawk, she fell on her ear in a pile of ruffled feathers.

Soon the rusty brown chicks traded their down for the pearl gray of the adult. Their blue-black wing quills were heavy now with blood as the great new flight feathers pushed out from the quills, light but strong feathers which would one day take them safely over the pine ridges which screened the ranch from their future world. I was sad as I watched them, almost afraid that they were growing up too soon.

But I couldn't keep them from changing. Their beaks grew iron-hard, long, saber-like, able to probe deep into the soil for worms. No longer caged, the four took over the ranch as though they owned the place. They had a sixth sense for trouble, but promptly got into it anyway.

"Eeny!" I yelped as Eeny stole a button off my shirt. "Meeny!" I squalled as Meeny hammered away at the laces of my shoes. "Miney!" I warned as Miney stabbed hard at the rivets of my Levis. Smaller than the rest, little Moe always came last, even for a scolding. He stood apart to enjoy the way the others were tormenting me, then, when my back was turned, stole my wallet and rushed off down the hill for a game of toss-the-wallet-into-the-spring.

"Moe!" I shouted, rushing after. But it was too late.

"Preeeeep!" Moe said happily as I fished my dripping wallet out of the drink.

The cranes on their black stilt-legs soon towered over their foster mothers, who stared at them in dismay, not quite knowing how to mother such giants though desperately determined to try. Inevitably, Eeny, Meeny, Miney, and Moe soon tired of being followed about by nervous Nellies who fussed and scolded most of the day.

Now almost two months old, it was a simple matter for the cranes to solve. They merely waded out into the middle of the pond, ignoring the frantic cackling of the hens, who ventured out ankle-deep then retreated to the safety of the shore. It was only when the cranes came out on the far side of the pond and wandered off that the hens returned to the regular life at the chicken house.

But a strange thing had happened. The cranes still had need of a parent symbol, someone who loomed

13

taller than they. To my dismay they turned all their attentions to me.

"Now there's a sight," my wife said as the four cranes marched single file behind me across the ranch. "If you ask me, there go five goofy birds."

All day long they followed me about my work, leaving no job uninspected, no moment unsupervised. They were my shadows, as hard to shake as a guilty conscience. As each night fell I felt a sense of relief, yet felt neglected too when I saw them silhouetted against the crimson pool the setting sun made in the pond, standing knee-deep in the chill waters, each one's wavelets lapping those of another.

But my rest was generally short-lived, for as darkness came and pools of light flowed out from the living room over the front porch, I would hear them calling to me in their loneliness. Then I would hear tiny footsteps, soft whisperings of feather against feather, the same rustlings my aged grandmother made years back, taking off her dozen petticoats in the darkness in the room next to mine. Sharp tappings of beaks against windowpanes. Click, bang, pling. Signals demanding that I look up from my book and notice them.

"It must be nice," my wife said once, "to be loved."

There was always much activity as they discovered

the moths fluttering toward the lights. Jackhammer blows struck against the panes as they made a late evening snack of moths, shredding the wings of those they didn't eat. "Preep, preep," insistent as a katydid in the grass. I refused to look up from my book as they called to me.

"You must be very talented," my wife remarked one evening. "You're reading that book upside down."

In the mornings the first squeak of a door hinge usually brought them running. One day I tried to slip out the back, but they were coming at a run. I rushed to the front door, but they had guessed my plan. Eeny, Meeny, Miney, and —— Wait! Where was Moe?

I rushed about the yard, expecting to find a pile of feathers where an eagle had dined on sandhill crane. Already I missed him. Why hadn't I been nicer to him? Poor Moe!

Suddenly I heard a rusty squawk from the basement of the ranch house. Moe had slid down the coal chute into the coalbin and now looked like a monstrous black raven. As I strode off I hid my head in my jacket, not wanting Moe to see me laughing. My four bosses came traipsing on behind to begin our day. Eeny, Meeny, and Miney, in that order, with poor Moe always coming last.

16

It wasn't that he couldn't keep up. Mostly he was so curious that he just couldn't resist investigating the world as he passed through it. Often before he ever got to his destination, he would meet the others coming back. Now and then the three larger cranes would find a luscious feast of grasshoppers, but by the time Moe rambled up, the last of the hoppers was eaten and he poked around in vain to see what the excitement had been about.

But sometimes, just sometimes, he found his own bonanza in the grass, and since none of the others gave him credit for much sense, he was able to finish off his meal all by himself without ever having to share.

As the long days of summer passed, I became more and more uneasy. Something seemed wrong with the cranes. I watched them carefully, trying to figure out what was different, what was missing. They were grown now, fully feathered and magnificent, but I had a feeling that I had left something out. Even though Sandy had laid the eggs which produced them, she went her lonely, haughty way, lacking the instincts for motherhood as is often the case when birds or animals are hand-raised by humans. "You hatched them," she seemed to say. "Now let's see you raise them." Suddenly I realized just how I had failed them. I had forgotten to teach them how to fly.

"You mean you know how?" my wife gasped, eying me suspiciously.

"Of course not," I snapped. "But in the wild their parents teach them to fly by running on ahead and teasing them into short flights. Watch how easy it is," I said, trying to prove my point. Spreading my arms and flapping them like wings, I rushed off across the meadow. Sure enough, calling excitedly, pleading not to be left behind, the foursome flapped their wings and followed.

"See?" I said proudly. "Now I'll take them up on the hill for a real flight."

With my four friends following behind, I sauntered up the hill. Now and then I would flap my arms and they would answer by flapping their wings. Clearly they were getting the idea.

At the top of the hill I turned. Without even a backward glance I spread wide my arms and rushed wildly down the hill. I heard squawks of excitement, the heavy beat of their pinion feathers as they flapped up over me. Eeny, Meeny, Miney, and now, yes, Moe, swept on past.

19

The excitement of the flight was catching. On and on I ran, striving to keep up. My fingertips were spread like pinions; I could feel the warm air slicing through. With . . . just . . . the . . . right . . . headwind . . . puff . . . puff . . . I could fly. Yes, yes, I could feel it. I was almost flying now, my feet scarcely touching the ground.

Down at the foot of the hill was a rim above a big sandpit. With a final burst of speed I spurted out into empty air. The cranes were just ahead of me. I was catching up. I was flying!

Crash! I ended up in a heap at the bottom of the pit. I heard a cough of embarrassment as I sat up. There in an automobile sat my banker, who had come out to inspect my ranch.

"He flew too near the sun," my wife said as she rushed up, "and the heat melted the wax on his wings."

The banker only stared.

"I was teaching my sandhill cranes to fly," I said, "and it worked. See, they are nowhere to be seen. You can't find them anywhere."

The banker got out of his car.

"Look out!" I shouted, but it was too late. The cranes had suddenly discovered that I was no longer flying with them and had come circling back through the trees. Branches crashed as they missed their

turns. Eeny, Meeny, and Miney managed to sweep over the banker's head. Moe would have made it too, had he been a foot higher up. As it was, he hit the banker right between the shoulder blades, and man and crane ended up in the dust.

If flying was easy for the young cranes, coming to earth gracefully was another matter. Time and again they approached the ground too fast and crashed in ungainly heaps. Afraid that they would injure themselves, I covered my eyes rather than watch them land. Soon, however, they learned to brake their forward speed with their wings and stretch out their long black legs to meet the racing ground with diminishing strides.

Once they had mastered all aspects of flight, they took over the skies as though they were their own. Like holdovers from the Pleistocene age, huge and primitive, they seemed to belong more to an age of dinosaurs than of rockets to the moon. Giant-winged, they floated in endless circles above the rich green meadows of the ranch. Having viewed my one attempt to fly, they seemed for now to accept the fact that I was doomed to stay on earth.

Sometimes they were but specks in the sky, circling in wide, effortless sweeps that took them from one mountainous horizon to another. But always Yamsi, with its broad, marshy pastures and shining, spring-fed waters, was the center of their world. However high they soared into the heavens, however often they were invisible to the eye of the earthbound, they seemed always to know my where-abouts. I had only to wave my arms to them and they would come planing down to land at my side.

"I think they are guarding us, and doing a pretty good job of it," my wife said.

"How so?" I asked a little testily.

"Come on, admit it now," she said with a smile. "Since they've been watching over us we haven't once been attacked by bandits!"

There were times when I might have preferred bandits to the cranes, but as I stopped my horse at some project or another down the valley, it was ever a source of wonder that they could check my movements from above and come gliding in from the invisible, eye-watering depths of azure sky to join me on the land below. I liked to imagine that they wanted to be sure I did the job right; more likely they were attracted by the worms and bugs I turned up in the moist earth in which I dug.

With saber-like bills they probed the banks of the irrigation ditches, ignoring me so completely as I mounted and rode off that I might have accounted for nothing in their lives. But then as I became smaller and looked more unprotected in the distance, there would come a great reawakening of their love. Thunderous wings in the air, and plaintive peeping accusations that I was trying to desert them. Then they would calmly resume their feeding until I was again part of the shimmering haze of the distance.

They had a hatred of airplanes bordering on the comic. Like their mother before them, the cranes picked up the sounds of jet aircraft long before they were audible to the human ear, and up they went to drive the plane from the skies. But somehow they never came to understand about the supersonic speeds of such aircraft. Invariably, by the time they gained a thousand feet, the jet had fled in terror and

was now south over the next county. But the satisfaction was there; they had responded to a territorial challenge as old as time. When they came soaring down to earth, they seemed drunk with pride that they had defended me from a horrible fate. By the time the next jet sounded on the horizon, they were ready for another flight in defense of their helpless friend.

Poor Moe. Often it took him so long to cease his concentration and get airborne that by the time he got properly located in the heights, the others would be back on the ground again, and he would sweep back and forth across the empty sky, miserable and alone.

Being solitary bothered him a great deal. Once a huge eagle roared down at them from high above as they flew. Eeny, Meeny, and Miney saw the danger from afar, and instinct made them fly a jagged, tumbling, evasive course back to earth. But Moe was dreaming along as usual when suddenly he glanced about to find his companions gone and the skies empty. Empty except for the diving eagle.

Taking the astonished eagle for a friend, Moe uttered a cry of delight and headed straight for him. With a massive clobbering of the air, the eagle braked his dive. Closer and closer came Moe, flying straight into the face of doom. It was more than the poor eagle could stand. Unused to being chased by his intended prey, he rocketed away. Moe, who was not to be left alone a second time, summoned all his strength and flew right after.

I could see the flashes of sunlight on the eagle's snowy head and tail as he twisted first right then left, trying to be free. At last, harried and bewildered, he sought refuge in a thicket until Moe, tired of trying to be friendly, came gliding in to join the others still hiding in the barn.

"Preep!" said Eeny when I found them, as though trying to tell me of their adventure.

"Preep!" said Meeny, as though agreeing to every detail.

"Preep!" said Miney, still frightened out of her wits.

But Moe said not a word. He was busy stalking my poor patient Irish setter Red, whom the cranes dearly loved to tease. Stealing up on the dog, who was sleeping in the hay, Moe seized him by the tail and held on for a crazy sleigh ride until Red dove under the hay manger and ran away. While the cranes all rushed about trying to find where the dog had gone, I used the resulting confusion to slip away myself and enjoy a few moments of peace without the cranes.

Having my waking moments supervised by the

four of them came to have distinct disadvantages. Whenever there had been unpleasant tasks to do, I would hide from my wife until the danger was past and she had done the job herself. But now the cranes played me right into her hands. She always knew my hiding place because there, patrolling patiently waiting for me to come out, would be Eeny, Meeny, Miney, and Moe.

They soon learned to cope with my trick of running in one door and passing out another to give them the slip. Now that they could fly, their strategy changed so that my disappearance into one door merely sent them airborne. Round and round the house they flew, peering into windows as they circled. Outside the front windows of the house would be Eeny, Meeny, and Miney, while from the back window I could see Moe, coming forever last.

Now that the cowboys were gone, it fell to me to break the colts.

"Be careful!" my wife advised.

"I have it all figured out," I replied. "I've locked Eeny, Meeny, Miney, and Moe in the barn. They can't possibly figure out the tricky new latch I invented for the door."

I saddled a wild-eyed colt, finally worked my way aboard, and stole a ride on him round and round the corral. What a relief it was to have the chance to ride off alone. From inside the barn I could hear the four cranes croaking endearments to me, but I ignored them. Soon my confidence got to running so far ahead of my ability that I let the corral gate swing open and headed out for the meadows. I had no sooner ridden down the lane and out into the middle of the field when I heard the flapping of distant wings. The cranes had mastered my latch, left the barn, and, straight as a group of surface-to-air missiles, they headed out to join me.

I stared at them in fascination. The pines seemed to stretch out to touch them as they passed above with measured beat, necks outstretched, solemn, dignified, effortless, inevitable as doom, cleaving the warm summer air with gentle grace. Between my knees, I felt my colt stiffen with terror. He flung his head high, his ears froze forward, and he trembled violently. Suddenly the cranes were upon us, churning the air with noisy, braking wings. My frightened colt panicked, plunged, squealed, and ducked his head to buck. I zigged when I should have zagged, and for one wild moment I flew like a crane, arms outstretched, solemn, effortless, while my horse careened away and stampeded for the barn.

Eeny pecked at my shoelaces; Meeny tweaked my ear lovingly; Miney speared at the battered brim of my hat; Moe tossed a stick in the air and bowed an invitation to the sandhill crane dance. They all pretended great concern, but you could be sure from the lights that gleamed in their mischievous eyes, that they were laughing at me one and all.

Since mischief in the form of the cranes could now come from land or air, nothing on the ranch was safe. My wife and I dared not relax any more; we were tense waiting for something to happen. I'm sure that Eeny, Meeny, Miney, and Moe meant well the day they demolished my wife's vegetable garden. They had been helping her pull weeds the day before and must have discovered that the clumps of roots often sheltered cool, moist bundles of earthworms, cut-

worms, and bugs. The next day they took over the project themselves. They not only pulled up all the weeds but all of the vegetables as well, and stacked both in haphazard rows in the August sun. Though they did rid the garden of pests, the crop also was demolished.

My wife sputtered in rage as she strode toward where I lazed in the shade of a pine tree. "You can just choose between me and those confounded cranes," she snapped. "If you refuse to pen them up, I'm going back to live with my mother. I hope Eeny, Meeny, Miney, and Moe know how to cook."

"I'm sorry about your garden," I said.

"My garden? I didn't know about my garden. What I was referring to was my lovely wash. Whiter than white. Now it's blacker than black. Marks from muddy beaks all over it as though they thought they were branding cattle. Stupid cranes!"

"While you're still mad, you'd better inspect your former vegetable garden," I said. "And I'll miss you around the ranch."

I was glad that she hadn't happened along an hour earlier. Moe had fallen into a pan of waste oil, and in his state of emotional distress was perhaps to be forgiven for marching right into the ranch kitchen to find me. In spite of my work with a scrub brush, the floor now had a pattern slightly different from the original.

Obviously she was prejudiced against the cranes. Only the week before, wearing new slacks, my wife had bent over to fix her shoe and forgotten that the cranes were standing behind her.

Now she stood with her hands on her hips and her mouth a straight line from corner to corner, letting me know that the cranes and I were in real trouble. "Remember those bulbs I ordered from Holland?" she said suddenly. "I always wondered why they never came up. I just remembered that the cranes watched me plant every one. If you want

35

me to stay, you'll just have to start building a cage."

I looked up in the sky. Far above us, the cranes were playing tag in and out of the clouds. They called down to me and their voices were brimful of love. Freedom! They had it. Man, harried and earthbound, could never know such ecstasy. My fingers crawled with excitement as I saw them sail high on a passing wind. I spread my fingers like pinion feathers and flapped my wings. My wife gave me a strange glance.

"Look at them," I said. "I just can't take away their freedom."

"Just think of what it will be like," my wife said. "Cooking your own food. Living in an empty house. Just you and your sandhill cranes."

As if sensing that they were being talked about, the big birds came gliding in, reaching for the racing ground with the long black landing gear of their legs. As they settled at my feet, Eeny speared a grasshopper from a ragwort plant and ate it eagerly; Meeny probed the ground for cutworms; Miney tried to eat the gold horse on my belt buckle; while Moe, whose landing had closely resembled a crash, tossed up a broken stick and tried to get me to dance.

But when I would not play with them, they moved away looking for Red. First they investigated the shady bowers beneath the willows, then they checked the lawn beside the house. They peered under all the cars and trucks, then flew noisily to the top of the haystack. Suddenly it occured to me that I hadn't seen the old dog all day.

A shadow flitted across my wife's face. "It's strange," she said. "Come to think of it, Red didn't come in to eat his supper last night."

With growing apprehension, we watched as the cranes searched for the dog until they had exhausted all his usual hiding places. We called and called. The pine trees echoed our voices and flung them back to us, but no Red appeared. Eeny, Meeny, Miney, and Moe flew off down the valley as though to check the rest of the ranch for their canine friend. That night even the cranes failed to return.

"He was such a nice old dog," my wife said, a mist dimming her eyes. She looked at me a little sheepishly. "After what I said, it might seem a little funny, but I even miss Eeny, Meeny, Miney, and Moe."

I rode down the meadows. The cattle grazed as usual along the river but somehow the valley had an empty look. Even my saddle horse, unused to traveling without cranes, stumbled over his big feet and spent entirely too much time staring about the horizon. He seemed almost to miss their company.

Then suddenly his ears pricked forward and he nickered. He glanced first at the meadows, then at the pine ridges that rose toward the mountains. I listened and far off I heard the calling of sandhill cranes, like trumpets from a distant land. I scanned the skies, but save for a gliding buzzard they were empty. The distant ratchettings were coming from the forest. Guided by the sound, I trotted up the hill.

Moments later I broke into a forest glade, and there were Eeny, Meeny, Miney, and Moe strutting back and forth before a massive rotten log. As I approached they called a greeting, then resumed their pacing. The dusty rotten log, filled with holes of wood-boring grubs, was scattered where it had been shredded by their probing beaks. "Come on, cranes," I said. "You've food enough at home without coming up here on a wild grub chase."

At the sound of my voice, a feeble whine and a muffled bark of joy came from the depths of the log. Eeny, Meeny, Miney, and Moe tipped back their heads and shouted their excitement. "Red!" I whooped and leaped from my horse. Perhaps it was a mouse, perhaps a squirrel that he had chased into the hollow log. In any event, he had crawled deeper and deeper into it until he was wedged tight, unable to back out. His barks must have been desperate, but there were no humans near. Then, circling over the forest, the cranes had heard.

I tore at the rotting wood with my hands, but

the wood resisted all my strength. Taking the lass rope off my saddle as I mounted my horse, I roped a projecting stub on the log, wrapped the other end of the rope around my saddle horn, and galloped away. As the horse hit the end of the rope there was a groan of splitting wood and a great crash as the old log flew open. In the red dust of his wooden prison, blinking at the unaccustomed light, the old red dog sat, none the worse for his experience. Without a backward glance at the cranes flapping after, he went trotting off toward the stream at the bottom of the hill.

That night my wife hugged the dog and put out an extra pan of food for the cranes. "I can always buy vegetables instead of growing them," she admitted, "but I guess it would be practically impossible to buy a sandhill crane."

In all nature there are few sights more spectacular than the dance of the sandhill cranes. It is a happy thing, a group thing, done at all seasons of the year but especially in the spring when the joy of living seems just too riotous to be contained. It can be a part of courtship and pairing, or a meaningless release of nervous tension. Quick as a blink the dance begins when one bird bows, seizes a handy stick, and tosses it into the air. Then, as others join, the bird leaps high, flapping its wings, ducking, twirling, bowing, stabbing the air and leaping high again. The action is so infectious that quickly the whole group shares in the lunacy.

The dance of the sandhill crane is one of the few things in life I'm rather good at, sort of a specialty of mine, you might say. My wife first noticed the change in me when she discovered that I was actually getting up early on my own accord without the usual nagging on her part, and for a time she thought I was doing something awfully important on the ranch. I would come in for breakfast tired enough to go back to bed and find myself some sort of a family hero for the hard work she thought I was doing.

In reality, once I had skipped out of the house, I dashed for the meadow outside the barn where my cranes were waiting for me, and once I had done the honors by tossing up the first stick, we would all get very excited and emotional, leaping high, flapping our wings, bowing and pirouetting, caught up in the ancient ritual.

There would be Eeny, Meeny, Miney, Moe, and Sandy as well as any wild sandhill crane who happened to be visiting. While these wild cranes kept their distance, they watched the whole proceedings with such interest that I came to believe they had come a long way out of their way just to watch me perform their dance. I was really that good.

But I had to limit my performance to early in the morning because I had a reputation to maintain, and it isn't wise to be seen doing that sort of thing when you are supposed to be a rough, tough rancher running a rough, tough ranch in the heart of rough, tough cattle country.

Always one to do things right, I built some nice little dusters of moulted crane feathers tied into bundles with strips of inner tube, which I held in each hand when I flapped to help me fly a little better. I kept these hidden in the barn because they would have been a little hard to explain.

I also had one special little bunch which I stuck into the back pocket of my Levis to simulate a tail, but this I lost one day when I forgot and wore it into town.

If I was the best dancer in the bunch, Moe was the worst. Frequently, it took Moe so long to get warmed up and into the mood of the dance that the rest of us were all through and Moe would have to dance all by himself. Although some of the cranes could flap their wings and jump clear over my back, Moe generally managed a wild leap that took him about one inch off the ground, but he was proud of it anyway. As a matter of fact, every time he took that wild leap, he just had to look around to make sure everyone was watching.

As summer became autumn, the voices of Eeny, Meeny, and Miney began changing to the glorious, stentorian trumpetings of the adult sandhill cranes, and they would terminate their dancing with a chorus loud enough to bring snow from the clouds. But when the others had quieted, Moe would step

44

forward, tip back his scrawny head, take a monstrous deep breath, open his beak wide, and go
"Preeep!" not much louder or more impressively
than when he'd first hatched from the egg.

It wasn't what you might call a flourishing summer. With my early morning activities, I wasn't
getting much sleep, and then too I had no hired
man to help me.

"You've got to hire a man," my wife finally said,
and so I drove into town to give it a try.

I went to the employment agency to interview a
cowboy. His face was craggy as a mountaintop
against a sunset, and his frown frozen hard. "How
many cows you run?" he asked.

I only run five hundred cows, but I could see that
he wanted to be impressed. "Couple of thousand," I
lied.

"Never did work for an outfit that small," he said.
"That few cows, how come you need a man?"

"My wife sprained her wrist," I said.

"Wife! You mean there's womenfolk around too?
On a ranch?"

"She sprained her wrist on the branding chute,"
I explained, trying to indicate that my wife was not
just any woman.

Distaste curled at the corners of his mouth.
"Branding chute! The ZX and all them good outfits

have plenty of good ropin' hands around for brandin' calves. They wouldn't have one of those gol-danged modern chute contraptions on the place. Them's just for poor outfits. And they wouldn't have a woman on the place neither. Only place I ever worked had a woman, you know what she did? She kept a canary bird in a cage. Think of that! A gol-danged bird on a cow ranch!" He got so red-faced just thinking about it that I thought he was going to have a stroke.

But it must have been a bad year for finding work, for when I rose in despair and started out the door, he followed me out. "Hey, wait a minute," he said. "Did you change your mind about hirin'?"

It was the proper time to explain about the sand-hill cranes, but somehow I didn't dare. I shrugged and loaded his saddle and gear into my car, dreading the moment of his arrival at the ranch.

I tried to slip old Walt into the bunkhouse as quietly as possible, but as we drove up, out of the skies dropped the whole noisy, clamorous gang of sandhill cranes.

"What in the name of thunder is them things?" Walt gasped.

"What things?" I asked. "Oh, those. Those are sandhill cranes, of course." I tried to sound very matter-of-fact, but my voice trembled.

"The heck they are," he said. "Why, they look just like a bunch of birds to me! Birds!" he snorted. "Thunderation! What's this cow business coming to?"

If it hadn't been sixty miles to town, old Walt would have hoofed it back. I should have shown him mercy and driven him, for the events that followed as Walt tried to adjust a half-century of habits and standards to our crazy cow ranch were disastrous.

Sensing Walt's dislike of birds, on his first morning the cranes kept him cornered for four hours in the outhouse. He then spent a whole week gathering a bunch of wild steers out of the brush, and was aces away from having them inside the corral gate when the cranes, descending upon him in a happy cloud, frightened his horse into bucking him off and with great satisfaction stampeded his herd away.

He hung his personal laundry out to dry only to have the cranes depart with odd mates for his socks, one of which still flies atop a hundred-twenty-foot ponderosa pine. They stood quite patiently and plucked the flap buttons off his long underwear, and then, for some reason known only to the cranes, decided that poor Walt was lonely and needed twenty-four-hour-a-day company, which had the effect of unnerving him completely.

The next great shock to his system was that I

asked him to milk the cow, a chore that any old desert cowboy would have thought beneath him. "The ZX never would have one of them dairy cows on the place," he informed me, hoping, no doubt, that I'd load the thing up and haul it into town. He wagged his old head dubiously. "Don't know what for you want the milk anyhow," he said. "The stuff ain't fit to drink. I knew a cowboy drank a glass of milk and you know what happened next time he tried to chew? He didn't have any teeth."

It was only when I promised never to tell anyone that he had milked a cow that Walt departed for the barn, the milk bucket held behind his body so no one could see his shame. I had just settled down to gloat over my good fortune when there was a roar of outrage from the barn and cranes flew everywhere, shrieking their delight. Walt had milked a good five inches into the bottom of the pail when one of the cranes grabbed the cow by the tail, and with one sidewinding kick the cantankerous animal drove Walt—stool, bucket, and all—out through the side of the barn.

As was inevitable, Walt discovered that just after sunrise every morning, the boss of this crazy outfit not only joined the cranes in a circle and talked to them as though they were humans, but bowed, pirouetted, tossed sticks into the air, and actually

danced with the long-legged birds. I tried to explain to him something of the rarity of the bird, that the crane dance was a sight seen by his ancestors as they crossed the plains in covered wagons.

"I thought this was supposed to be a cow outfit," he grumbled as he headed for the bunkhouse. "Ain't no end to the shame a man has to put up with when he gets old."

As autumn came the situation became more explosive. I lost weight under the emotional impact of Walt's disapproving glance. I began snapping at my wife, and was thinking of trading the ranch off to seek another way of life.

Then one morning I chanced to come around the corner of the barn and there was old Walt himself, hat in hand, gray hair flying. He stood in a circle with the cranes, a big silly grin on his face, and with tremendous flaps of his arms, he was dancing up a storm.

7

Autumn on a cattle ranch is a busy time. Once the summer's hay crop is snug and dry in the barns, it is time to gather the cows and calves off the vast ranges, and wean the calves from the cows so the calves can be sold.

Although Eeny, Meeny, Miney, and Moe lacked red crowns, they resembled adult cranes in every other way. More and more I left them on their own. They spent long hours flying circles high above the ranch. Sometimes as I clambered down off my tired horse to eat my lunch on a distant meadow, they would descend out of nowhere to keep me company while I ate, quarreling over bread crumbs or simply preening, happy that I could spare them some time.

Along the quiet river running through the ranch, the aspens and willows changed to gold, then turned bare as the banks beneath pulled down the yellow blanket for their winter's sleep. Frost turned the grasses brown and sere. Along the marshes, ducks and geese by the hundreds rested their tired wings for the next lap southward.

There was a hint of snow in the sky. Even old Walt huddled a little longer over his morning coffee before riding out over the ranch. In the four young cranes the instincts for migration were building. I saw in them a nervousness, an innate restlessness that made them look often to the leaden skies. More and more they took to the air, spending long lazy hours endlessly circling, strengthening their wings, feeding in some solitary marsh on insect prey, but returning regularly to check my whereabouts, as though they feared that I might migrate without them to a warmer climate.

I could always set them off on an adventure by running along the ground flapping my "wings."

Clamoring happily in excitement, they would start in pursuit, thinking perhaps that at long last their hopelessly stupid human friend had learned how to fly. They would be over my head, airborne and soaring, before they realized that I had failed again. Once they felt the sweetness of the air they were understandably reluctant to set wings again for the long glide home, but instead would soar higher and higher, circling on effortless wings, riding some invisible up-draft I would never be able to share.

My original intent in raising Eeny, Meeny, Miney, and Moe was to find ways to raise sandhill cranes in captivity for release into the wild fully able to care for themselves. While my four could fly and feed themselves, they were not afraid of people, and not all people might treat them as well as I. Their tameness pointed up the fact that if I wanted to produce wild and wary cranes to supplement the diminishing numbers of the wild flock, I would have to raise the young behind screens so that they never saw humans or associated man with food. (In time I used this system successfully and at last was able to put sandhill cranes back into the environment as fully wild migrating birds.)

But there was still much that Eeny, Meeny, Miney, and Moe could teach me. Little was known of the migratory habits of the cranes, or where the southern Oregon cranes spent the winter. Being tame, my pets were bound to create a sensation along their migratory route and perhaps leave a record of their passage. Much as I dreaded the lonely life without them, I knew I must let them go for what I could learn from them.

One morning in November when the meadows were dull and drab and the scent of snow was in the air, Eeny, Meeny, Miney, and Moe came sailing down, not to say good-bye but to take me with them. The strange impulse of migration was gnawing hard at them, but there was an urgency to their devotion as though they sensed that if I did not now learn to fly with them, I would inevitably starve. Again and again, as I had once taught them, they tried to teach me to fly. Again and again they came back to me out of the southern skies, came back and called me, entreating me to go along.

A cold wind was settling down off the black, forboding hills, and the somber sky was sullen with the approach of winter. Eeny, Meeny, Miney, and Moe called excitely, tugged at my clothes with their beaks, ran and leaped into the air, calling endearments as they flew low over my head.

Higher and higher the young cranes rose into the vast sky until they were like light ashes above some far-off campfire, a strange mobile of the gods.

Then as I watched sadly, they began to slip southward over the ridge and the next valley's glades,
and they were gone. A snowflake caught on my eye-
lash and seemed to take forever melting. The valley
was lonely and empty now without them. Only a
few hardy ducks and geese sat humped and silent
along the frozen edges of the river.

The snows came heavy and thick from the lower-
ing clouds, covering my valley with a white shroud.
Day after day we harnessed the draft teams and
hauled wagonloads of hay out to the wintering

cattle on the meadows. In the basement of the ranch house the rough-skinned toads circled the furnace and sat out the winter in shrunken overcoats. Their eyes glistened like tiny ruby fires in the half-light. With each snowbound day a slow but certain step toward spring, I stayed at home and waited, along with the dormant insects and butterflies hibernating in the curtain folds.

I had asked the Bureau of Sports Fisheries and Wildlife biologists at the various refuges to the south to notify me in case there were any reports of my tame cranes. Although a few wild flocks of cranes were reported wintering in some of the marshy areas of central California, just where Eeny, Meeny, Miney, and Moe had disappeared to was anyone's guess.

I had many worries. Even though sandhill cranes are protected by law, the laws could not protect them from fools with guns, from pesticides, power lines, pollution of water and air. I thought that perhaps the birds might land at some farmhouse on the way and beg for food. The presence of four giant birds would be bound to attract comment in the local newspapers; how often in life really does one get to rub elbows with a sandhill crane? But month after month went by and I heard never a word. It was as though Eeny, Meeny, Miney, and Moe had flown too high and landed on the moon.

Spring came and the snow melted, leaving the land tinged with the first green of the year. The wild cranes came back from migration and set up housekeeping in the marshes along the river. Day after day I watched and waited, but Eeny, Meeny, Miney, and Moe did not appear.

And then one day as I drove to town for groceries, dressed in my Sunday best, I spotted four sandhill cranes right in the middle of a roadside barley field. To the west of me was the vast calm of Klamath Lake, to the east rose steep rocky hills. Here and there the highway cut across shallow bays which had been drained and turned into rich agricultural lands. Never before had I seen sandhills so close to a road.

I slammed on the brakes, careened over to the shoulder, parked the car, and jumped out.

The effect was electric. Behind me brakes squealed, and traffic stopped to see if an avalanche was starting on the hills above. Drivers got out of their cars for a welcome stretch, and watched me as I waded the muddy morass of the field. Their laughter was coarse, derisive.

"Let them make fools of themselves," I thought. "Wait until I walk right up to Eeeny, Meeny, Miney, and Moe. I'll show them a sight. Maybe I'll even do

a sandhill crane dance out there in front of everyone." Just then the mud sucked away one of my shoes and in my excitement I failed to retrieve it.

"That guy must be nuts," a woman said angrily. All up and down the line, people started calling, "Cuckoo! Cuckoo!"

"Somebody call the cops," a man said. "That guy needs a ride to the booby hatch."

At that point I tripped on a buried root and fell face down in the mud. Far down the highway, north and south, more cars were stopping.

The cranes were closer now, eyeing me suspiciously. "Come on, boys," I called. "It's me! Your old pal! The unflying one."

"He's talkin' to them birds," a woman said. "Hey, Mabel, he's talkin' to them herons."

And then another voice came loud and clear. "Looky thar, Ma! Them birds is flying away!"

And flying away they were without so much as a backward glance. Rooted deep in the black peat muck, I had a good look at them as their long slow wing-beats bore them skyward. They were not my birds at all but two old mated pairs. Carrying my one remaining shoe, I slunk barefoot back to my car.

"Hey, Ma," a child's voice asked. "What do you reckon that man's going to do with just one shoe?"

Mud and all, I flopped into the car as a state policeman tried valiantly to get the traffic moving again.

"What caused the tie-up?" he asked me as I eased by.

"Some crazy guy," I said. "He was running out there in the mud with his Sunday suit on chasing birds."

How often during that endless spring did I stand in the greening meadows at Yamsi, forgetful of my work, watching the skies until the brightness dimmed my eyes with tears? Once I caught old Walt sadly putting out a pan of feed for them. "Figured it might bring them home," he said sheepishly. But still they didn't come.

How often did my imagination fancy four specks on high; how often did I thrill to crane voices in the faultless blue as wild cranes circled north, mere specks, migrating high, headed for some far-off valley not my own? I visited every known crane marsh for miles around, waded out toward the astonished denizens and called and called. But in the end the cranes always flew away. Did they really exist, my four? Had some storm borne them out to sea and dropped them exhausted but still trusting upon the angry winter ocean? Had some hunter shot them in panic as they walked toward him to beg for food? Had I, by sending them off tame into an often hostile world, merely signed their death warrants? I clung stubbornly to the thought that someone in the world had to know what happened to them if only I could find that person.

I wrote off a flurry of letters to newspapers, to wildlife people, asking for any information as to the possible whereabouts of my sandhill cranes. And slowly, clue by clue, the story of their migration began to unfold.

First the maintenance man at a high school football field, whom I met quite by accident, recalled chasing three cranes off his field in November, and watching them fly south right over the main street of his small southern Oregon town. Three cranes instead of four, but maybe he hadn't counted right. Then an ornithologist in far-off Michigan wrote that he remembered reading an Audubon Society field-note stating that in December three tame birds, tentatively identified as great blue herons, had caused a sensation on Bodega Bay near Santa Rosa, California, some five hundred miles south of me. Great blue herons resemble sandhill cranes, but seldom get tame. The chance that these could be my birds seemed slight, but again I sent out a flood of letters.

The editor of the Santa Rosa *Press Democrat* tracked down a write-up on the "herons" in his December issues, but there the trail vanished. A host of people had read about them in the paper and gone down to see them on the beach, but one morning they were gone and no one knew where. The editor requested information from any of his readers who might know the whereabouts of the three vanished birds.

Day after day I watched for letters in the mail, but none came. The trail seemed cold, the episode forgotten. I began to have great doubts. Were they really my birds? Why had the witnesses reported only three birds instead of four? Maybe they were blue herons after all.

Then suddenly, when I had almost lost hope, a letter came from an Air Force sergeant stationed at a small airfield north of San Francisco. Accustomed to watching jets land, he had been astonished to see three giant birds drop out of the sky to use the runway. And when they seemed to take over the airstrip as their very own, calling in anger at any jet that landed, he was even more dumbfounded. He was about to chase the cranes back into the sky for fear they might cause an accident when the birds walked calmly over to him and untied his shoelaces.

From then on the cranes had found a friend. All winter long, he fed them and kept them out of mischief. But when spring came, the commanding general himself called the sergeant in for a little visit. Not only had the cranes pulled up the general's flowers, but they had been pecking holes in the window screens at headquarters and frightening the secretaries half to death. With this blunt court-martial, the birds were convicted and sent off to the Fleishacker Zoo in San Francisco.

Now their migratory trip was ended, for they were placed in a large roofed aviary with several other species of crane. The time for their return north came and went. How desperately they must have wanted to return to the green meadows at Yamsi, but even with the nervous instincts of migration hard at them, they were caged up tight and could not escape.

I rushed off a letter to the zoo officials, explaining my crane research program and the probability that

the three cranes in their possession were actually the Yamsi birds.

Their reply was disappointing, though understandable. Since great rivalry exists between zoos, and no other zoo in the country could boast such a prize as three tame sandhill cranes, the officials were not about to give them up to some crazy Oregon rancher who claimed to have raised them from eggs. They would let me have them only if I could prove that they were rightfully mine. That chance must have seemed to them awfully slim.

I did have doubts. There were three birds now instead of four. I hadn't banded them for fear the bands might catch and hurt them as they crawled through a barbed wire fence. There were no distinguishing features except facial expressions, and those would be a little hard to explain to an irate and suspicious zoo director who would tend to dislike me even before he met me.

"Well, looky here, sir. This crane always did remind me of my mother-in-law. Here's a snapshot. See the resemblance?" I would be lucky to stay out of the local jail.

But when I grew discouraged, I thought of the cranes' love of freedom, and how lonely the ranch was without them. And I had yet many things to learn about sandhills which they might teach me.

If I used the cranes as a nucleus for a captive breeding flock, I might refine my slipshod techniques, explore many behavioral mysteries such as the belligerence crane chicks have for each other while in the downy stage, or the tendency for adult cranes to change the color of their feathers before the nesting season by actually using their beaks to apply natural dyes from the marshes. An understanding of diets, feather moults, and disease prevention would also be important if I were to hope to reestablish the sandhill crane in marshes where it hadn't been seen in years.

Gathering courage, I phoned the zoo director and told him that while the cranes didn't have any markings I could identify, I was certain that they could identify me.

Hanging up before he could say, "Don't bother to come!" I threw the back seat out of the family car, waved to my startled wife, and headed for San Francisco more than five hundred miles to the south. To lessen my loneliness, I stopped and bought a little Irish setter puppy at a farmhouse along the way, and settled him in the front seat for company.

The farther I drove, the more I was assailed by doubts. How mortified I would be if the cranes turned out to be strangers. Why were there three birds instead of four? If one of the cranes had vanished on the flight south, would it be Eeny, Meeny, Miney, or Moe? And if it were Moe, the smallest and weakest and most dependent upon me, would the others, fed for some months by a series of strange keepers, demonstrate visibly that they recognized a man they hadn't seen for eight months, and then in a far different environment?

At the zoo the officials were startled by the swift appearance of what had until then been only the writer of a letter and a voice on the telephone, but now turned out to be a tired, harried, six-foot-five-inch cowboy, complete with Stetson hat and high-heeled boots.

"You've parked your car in my private parking space," the director said. He promptly turned me over to the nice old keeper of the birds and disappeared for the day. In my impatience I practically threw the keeper into my car, to be licked by the lonesome setter puppy, and we drove off to see the cranes.

The sandhills were being kept in a huge aviary filled with all kinds of birds, from storks to herons. A crowd of some sixty people thronged the outside of the collection. My heart skipped a beat as I recognized Miney, then Eeny, and Meeny. But even in my joy I tried desperately to count one more, to see my little friend Moe hidden somewhere in a far corner. But there were three sandhill cranes and only three.

As I had somehow dreaded all along, it was poor Moe that was missing.

Dejectedly the three birds wandered back and forth, not paying the slightest bit of attention to my approach through the crowd. They had seen enough people at the zoo to be bored by them. According to the keeper, Miney had lost an eye by flying up in fright against the roof one night when zoo officials, during a late inspection, had turned on the lights. One after another the cranes fluffed their feathers, then all seemed to doze. My heart sank; after all those months I was only another face in the constantly changing crowd.

The bird keeper glanced at his watch as though his time had been wasted. I had to do something quickly to make them remember or the birds were lost to me forever. Slipping to the rear of the crowd, I called to them as I had often called at feeding time.

Inside the sleepy aviary, pandemonium broke loose. Eeny, Meeny, and Miney straightened up to full height, called loudly to each other, and stared at the crowd. Then suddenly they spotted me. Shrieking wildly, they left the other groups and flung themselves at the heavy wire between us. A short swarthy man in a knitted cap stared in disbelief. "Say, mister," he said excitedly. "I think them birds knows you!"

As the crowd watched, mystified, and the keeper stood by in a state of shock, I backed my car into the compound, let the cranes out of their cage, and pushed them into the back seat of the car. Then while the frightened puppy barked at the cranes from behind the steering wheel, and the cranes investigated their new environment, I shouted my good-byes and thank yous out the window and departed for the ranch.

The drive north must have been one of the strangest bird migrations in history. I am a sagebrush type of driver, and the perils of navigating through the heart of rush-hour San Francisco with three lovesick sand-hill cranes pacing the back seat, and an excited Irish setter puppy up front, made for chaos. The puppy stuck his head out of one window and the cranes took another, enjoying the streaming of the wind. But they attracted the very traffic I longed to be rid of.

Getting lost wasn't hard; it was easy. Suddenly I heard the scream of a runaway siren and a policeman shot out from nowhere, forcing me to the curb. "Where do you think you're going, cowboy?" the officer snapped, appearing with a scowl at my window.

"We're sandhill cranes, Officer, and it's spring. We're migrating north to Oregon."

Starved as they were for the sound of my voice, the cranes tilted back their heads and hollered to break eardrums.

"Well, everyone else is migrating south. This is a one-way street. Follow my car; the station is just around the corner."

Eeny tried to pick the pencil from behind the policeman's ear, while the rest concentrated on his notebook. "And hurry," he snapped, getting into his car and slamming the door.

I really tried my best to follow him, but I'm just not that good a driver in city traffic. First one unmannerly car then another shoved between us, then I was in the wrong lane and couldn't turn when he did without breaking the law. When I looked out my window he had his down and was shouting something about his book; somehow I never got to see him again. Moments later we were driving across the bay bridge bound for Oregon.

I soon found what he meant about a book. The cranes had somehow managed to steal his citation book and now they tore the pages out by the beakful and danced with them in the breeze.

We had a little trouble getting through the tollgate. Every time I would try to hand the timid tollkeeper a quarter, Meeny would try to intercept it. Rather than lose a hand, the man waved us on. I threw the money out the window anyway and fled.

On and on we went. My passengers drank in the sights, chortling merrily out the window like children on a bus. Cars honked; people stared, waved, laughed, and frowned. At last a car signaled us off the road. "Hey, mister," the man called. "Some big birds flew in the back of your car!"

I was so relieved to be out of the city at last that I stayed there a whole hour giving him a free lecture on sandhill cranes, and when I left the cranes had another friend. The farther we got from the city, the friendlier and more curious people became.

At length, however, we ran into a different type. As we parked in a drive-in restaurant and waited to be served, a frowny-faced woman who looked as though her last smile had been a decade before, pulled in next to us. For some time she sat stubbornly staring straight ahead, refusing to acknowledge the cranes at her elbow. The fact that she could sit next to

that gang and not react seemed to indicate that she felt such notice beneath her dignity.

Holding the menu over my shoulder, I pretended to consult with the birds. "Say, Miney," I said. "How about some sardines on toast?"

At the sound of my voice the cranes became excited, tweaked my ear as though in agreement, and called loud enough to shatter glass. I held a glass of water over my shoulder and the three drank thirstily, tipping their heads back to the ceiling. Once more I consulted them, nodding my head in bored agreement. By now the poor woman was leaning so heavily toward us, striving to catch every word, that the door latch gave way, spilling her out onto the pavement. Shoving her hat back on her head, she leaped in, slammed the car door, rammed into reverse, and shot off to look for a quieter place to eat.

As we migrated northward, the cranes became more and more joyous, as though they realized perfectly that they were headed home and were eager to get there. Had I turned them loose, they probably would have flown home by nightfall, but I couldn't risk disaster. I had lost poor Moe and his loss made me cherish the others even more fondly.

Yamsi is screened from the rest of the world by mountains so there could not have been much chance for them to recognize the land through which we now passed. And yet the closer we came to the ranch, the more frantic they became.

Calling loudly, they tweaked my ears with saber beaks until they drew blood, peered out one window then the next. Every trip between windows meant crossing over one another, wings spread for balance, jockeying for position, croaking peevishly at me for driving so slowly and at the other drivers for getting in our way.

The last twenty miles of bumpy, dusty road seemed interminable. Even though it was hot, to protect my

battered ears I had to drive with my hat pushed down over them. Every minute or two, one of the cranes would step on the restless setter pup, who complained loudly. At the top of the hill overlooking my valley, all the cranes began to dance and flap their wings.

Caught up with the excitement, the pup chose this moment of moments to be carsick, and in the ensuing melee I managed to get a mouthful of feathers, for all three cranes hopped over into the front seat. I got only an occasional look at the road and that through wings. Miney somehow got a toenail caught in my gray flannel trousers, slashing them wide open from belt to cuff.

In desperation I skidded to a stop near the ranch house and pushed open the door. Dog and cranes bounded over the full length of me in their eagerness to be free. Once out, the pup looked bewildered, but the cranes called loudly as though to old friends, walked a few stiff steps, then took to the air for a rapid circle of the house. For one mad moment I thought they were going to fly back to the zoo. Instead they glided down over the willows to visit old Walt and the gang they had left behind almost a full year before.

In vain I listened for Moe's rusty call, hoping that he had returned to Yamsi in my absence to welcome us home, hoping that the little crane who always came last would somehow materialize from the skies above Taylor Butte and descend to make my family complete. Eeny, Meeny, and Miney took over the ranch as though they had never been away, but still Moe did not come.

10

With work piling up at the ranch, I couldn't wander around forever in a daze watching for Moe. But the fact that I had been able to come up with three of the four cranes against desperate odds made me more than ever hopeful of finding the remaining bird. I had tended to disregard the report by the football-field maintenance man because he had reported three birds instead of four. Now his report became impor-tant since it indicated that Moe had probably become separated from the others in the first few miles of flight. Because of Moe's character I doubted that he would proceed very far south on his own, so I decided to look for him closer to home.

It was an old Klamath Indian who gave me my first clue about Moe. Dressed in Levis and a battered Stetson, he had been out hunting deer on the neighboring reservation when his pickup developed engine trouble. I gave him a ride in my car, which was still a litter of crane feathers and puppy hair from the trip. "Sorry about the mess," I apologized. He picked up a crane feather and looked at it thoughtfully as we drove.

"From a sandhill crane," he said. "Last fall I saw four of them fly over my place along the Sprague River. I shot one out of the air with my deer rifle, but he came down on the far side of the stream and ran off through the brush. Must have just tipped his wing, because he stayed along the marshes there most of the winter."

I stared at him in angry amazement, then realized that he was only doing what his father had done before him, and his action represented failure on my part to educate the local people as to the rarity of the birds.

"Where's the bird now?" I asked, trying to keep the car on the road.

"Don't know," he said. "Most likely a coyote got it. I haven't seen that crane in over two months."

I tried to get a grip on myself. Don't break your heart, I thought. Here you are getting all steamed up over a story by a stranger and the chances of the bird being Moe are one in a thousand.

Before I drove him to his log cabin beside the river, I subjected the old man to a long lecture on the rarity of sandhill cranes, and pointed out that every remaining bird is important to the species. Filled with remorse, the kind old man took me to the exact bend of the river where he had last seen the crane.

I had work to do at the ranch, but I ignored it. Instead I wandered through the marshes, calling for Moe, looking for any sign of him. I was excited to find crane tracks in the dried mud, old droppings, a few faded feathers lost in preening, but there was nothing fresh, nothing to suggest that the crane was still alive.

Here the river was swift and deep. Unable to fly, the crane could not have crossed without drowning. If the crane were Moe and he wanted to come home, he would have been held back by the stream. As I moved upstream, the signs became less frequent.

I had almost given up when I found a bonanza of tracks, sharply etched in the mud but old. Here a crane had spent some time, weeks perhaps, probing the soft mud, preening his moulting feathers on the bar of sand which jutted out into the stream. The bird had spent all its time on one side of the river; obviously, it couldn't fly. The Indian's story was being borne out. I thrilled to the hope that I might be coming closer and closer to Moe.

Until the water dropped in July, the sand bar had been flooded, and all tracks would have been washed away. Tracks on the bar indicated that the bird had been here within the past two months, perhaps waiting for the water to drop. Now in late summer, the water had receded to the point where the bird could easily wade across.

I spent another day searching for tracks along the far shore, then, toward evening, I found faint footprints and a single feather. I knew then that the bird had crossed. But now, instead of staying along the river, the tracks showed that he had gone stalking off into the forest where there was little chance that a flightless crane could survive. As if to accent the hopelessness of my search, a chorus of coyotes sounded from the ridges above the river, and a huge spotted lynx cat leaped down from a stub where he had been watching me, and was gone. Time and again I searched the area but once more, Moe had vanished into the unknown.

Since I could not further neglect the ranch, I threw myself into my work, preparing for the haying season. Eeny, Meeny, and Miney ignored Moe's absence as they had once ignored his presence. They took over the ranch as though they had never been away. Appreciating them as never before, I let them rule my life. But sometimes as I watched them sailing lazily above the ranch, playing hide-and-seek among the clouds, I would count them and for one startling moment there would be four instead of three. It was almost as though Moe lived up there behind the clouds and came out only to play with the others. But when they set their wings for home, alas, there were always only three.

And now, when Eeny, Meeny, and Miney flew around the ranch house looking for me, I would whirl as the three flew past the front windows, hoping as in the old days to see Moe flying past the rear. But all I saw were pine boughs dancing in the wind.

As winter approached, I busied myself building a pen for the cranes, a wooded compound where they not only could be restrained from migrating south, but could be protected from any hungry winter predators that might wander out of the forest. There was a time when the instincts of migration were hard at them, but soon the nervousness passed and they settled down to the routine of winter living. As the first snows came gently down, covering their world with a shroud of white, Eeny, Meeny, and Miney moved to the shelter of a pine thicket near the stream to wait out the storm, while I stole guiltily away to the comfort of a roaring fire in the Yamsi hearth, there to dream of spring when I could once more begin my crane research program.

More and more I became resigned to Moe's loss. During his short life he had done his share to help me understand his species. From his first gasping moments out of the shell, Moe had had to struggle hard for existence in a world where only the strongest are meant to survive. It was nature's way. The three strong cranes would carry on. I must learn to go on without him. But, staring into the flames, I appreciated the joys he had given me and knew that I would always watch the skies for him and wonder where in all that lonely expanse of forest, river, mountain, and desert he had come to rest. Someday, perhaps, someone would show up to tell his story.